A WEEK IN THE LIFE OF
THE DONKEY SANCTUARY

A WEEK IN THE LIFE OF THE DONKEY SANCTUARY

Elisabeth D. Svendsen MBE

Whittet Books

(Facing title) *Aerial view of Slade House Farm.*

First published 1988
© 1988 by Elisabeth D. Svendsen

Whittet Books Ltd,
18 Anley Road, London W14 0BY

Design by Richard Kelly

The Donkey Sanctuary is at Sidmouth,
Devon EX10 0NU

British Library Cataloguing in Publication Data
Svendsen, Elisabeth D.
A week in the life of the donkey sanctuary.
1. Donkey Sanctuary
I. Title
639.9'79725   SF361
ISBN 0-905483-61-8

Typeset by Systemset Composition, NW2

Printed in Hong Kong by South China Printing Co.

The photographs appear by kind permission of the following:
Ian Cook/*People Weekly*, p.84/85; June Evers, p.15, p.48,
p.49(2), p.74; R. and S. Harrington, p.8, p.13, p.16, p.21,
p.27, p.71, p.72, p.92(2); Dorothy Morris, p.6/7, p.12(left),
p.14, p.19, p.22, p.23, p.25, p.26, p.28/29, p.31, p.33, p.35,
p.37, p.39, p.40, p.42/43, p.45, p.46(2), p.52/53, p.54,
p.55(3), p.56, p.57, p.59, p.60/61, p.63, p.64, p.66/67, p.69,
p.70, p.78/79, p.81(2), p.82, p.83, p.86, p.87, p.89, p.90,
p.91, p.95; Nicholas Toyne, p.2, p.10, p.11, p.12 (right).

INTRODUCTION

Over the years the Donkey Sanctuary has developed from one donkey called Naughty Face to one of the largest animal charities in the United Kingdom, with a donkey population at the moment of over three thousand. I little thought, way back in 1968, when I bought my first donkey, that donkeys were to play such a vitally important role in my life and were, in fact, to alter my circumstances almost beyond belief. Many people ask me why I have devoted my life to donkeys, and why I am prepared to work almost every hour of the day and week on behalf of the donkeys, and all I can reply is that, to me, it is not a job; hours are not there to be counted, and I love the work so much that weekends become part of a normal week and the weeks seem to run into each other. Somehow I just spend all my time happily looking after the donkeys and their interests.

As the charity has grown, my job has become more rewarding and interesting. The problems facing our charity now have not altered all that much from those in the early days; it has always been our policy to put the donkeys first, second and third, and it seems that everything else has to slot into place after these priorities. However, there is obviously an enormous amount of work to be done on the administration side to pay for our ever-increasing number of donkeys and to cope with the worldwide interest we have created and to keep the momentum going to ensure that donkeys' futures, not only in this country but abroad, are properly catered for. I felt it would be interesting to write a book in the form of a diary for one week in the life of the Donkey Sanctuary to try to give some impression of the problems that face us during an average working week and to give you some insight into our work. I have started on a Saturday because, to me, this is when a new week starts as the staff's working week ends on Friday and relief staff come in over the weekend.

Elisabeth D. Svendsen MBE
June 1987

Mares in the field by the sea.

SATU

RDAY

*'I was horrified to
see their condition.'*

Saturday starts for me at 7.45 a.m. when I arrive on the yards to see the donkeys at Slade House Farm for the first time that morning. Norman, the night watchman, always meets me and passes over any information on events during the night and on this particular Saturday he took me straight to the stable of two donkeys who had arrived the night before. It had been very dark when they arrived and the donkeys were tired and unsettled and we had put them straight into a large airy loose-box with plenty of straw as bedding and with ample hay and water for the night and left them to recover. I had, however, noticed that the feet of one looked terrible and that the other donkey looked in a fairly poor condition. Norman's concern was evident and I was somewhat horrified to see the state of the two donkeys. Their names were Lucy and Katy and they were obviously going to need special help over the weekend.

As I walked down through the yards to go back to the office, the Saturday staff were coming in and the donkeys were already getting excited at the thought of breakfast. All the geriatric donkeys who live at Slade House Farm get individual attention at breakfast time and now the individual feeding bowls were being put across the yard for those who have little or no teeth left and spend a long time chewing or sucking their morning feed. The more able donkeys are fed in their own boxes and they too had their heads out over the doors watching in anticipation as their turn for feeding came nearer.

Opening up the offices, I went in and immediately took off the messages which had come on the ansaphone after the evening staff had left at 10 p.m. the previous night. As usual, this contained about seven messages and, fortunately, on this particular morning there were no emergency calls. There was, however, a call from the Sunday *Observer* magazine confirming they were going to meet me the following week and also one from a Dr

Getting ready for the arena.

(Right) *Buffalo: the sanctuary's favourite.*

McGregor who wanted to come and see me on Saturday afternoon with regard to the Slade Centre.

I then went up to my office and almost immediately Walter, the postman, arrived with an enormous bag of post, the result of the Donkey Sanctuary's Newsletter which had gone out the previous week. As usual Walter insisted on tipping the whole bag out on my office floor and putting each pile of mail up on my desk, obviously pleased to feel that he was helping even in a small way. Our local postmen really are quite magnificent and make a great effort to get the mail out to us early in the morning as they know how important it is for us to get through the routine work so that we can get on with the donkey work. Once he had left I settled down to open the post—or at least all those letters which looked as though they had important information—and packaged the others back into hundreds so that the office could sort them out properly on Monday

morning when I had a full staff. There were approximately 800 letters to go through so, as you can imagine, it took some time. Halfway through my sister, Pat Feather, Principal of the Slade Centre arrived; she had popped in to make sure that the contractors laying the new floor in the centre, which had been badly damaged in the floods, had in fact turned up and done the job properly and she was extremely pleased with the results. She also brought some lovely photographs taken the week before when the handicapped children had done a wonderful display two days running at Devon County Show and we both spent some minutes looking at these. Pat then went back to the Slade Centre and I got on with the post. By 9.30 it was all sorted out and I could deal with the many problems that had arrived on my desk. Before I could do so, however, the door opened yet again and in came Brian Bagwell, my deputy administrator. As he was on holiday that week I had not expected him,

(Far left) *'Walter tipped the whole bag out on the floor.'*

(Left) *Penny with treated face.*

(Right) *Kenya entry on display at the Devon County Show.*

but, like me, he finds it very difficult to keep away and I was delighted to see him as we had been having quite a problem with one of the buildings on which Brian is an expert and this problem too was soon resolved.

Neil Harvey, who looks after the new arrivals and isolation donkeys, then arrived at my door and asked me if I would come out and look at Lucy and Katy, the two donkeys who had arrived the night before and about whom I was already very concerned. I went out with him and we brought the donkeys out into the yard to have a good look at them. I was quite appalled at their state. They were mother and daughter, the mother being at least forty-three and the daughter in her late thirties and neither were in a good condition. The mother was thin and generally poor, her coat being rubbed, and the daughter had extremely bad feet. They were both very tired and I learnt that they had been giving donkey rides up to a very short time before they were sent in by our inspector, although their owners had appreciated the problem and, realizing they could no longer cope, had relinquished them to us. I was so shocked by their condition that I left a message for John Fowler, our senior veterinary surgeon, to look at them on the beginning of his rounds as soon as he came in, to determine whether we dared cut their feet that day or whether we should wait yet another day to give them time

to settle in to their new surroundings.

I also had a look at two donkeys who were in the next-door stable, called Penny and Tuppence. These two donkeys had large scars on the sides of their faces because they had been tethered on a golf course and left so long that the head collars had actually embedded themselves into the skin and they had to be cut off by our inspector when she collected them. Apart from this the donkeys seemed in reasonable condition and were extremely friendly and enjoyed the extra fuss we gave them. I then walked off around the sanctuary, as Saturday is a lovely time to stop and talk quietly to the donkeys without being called constantly back to the telephone in the office as so often happens on a weekday. Eeyore never fails to gallop up to meet me at the rails and it was lovely to see Buffalo, one of our favourite donkeys, looking so fit and well and happy in his new quarters. We had just opened a new section of boxes, each with its own separate run-out area; here we managed to get most of the 'beach' donkeys, who have come from Blackpool and other beaches at various stages, together and they thoroughly enjoy these specially built quarters which have infra-red lamps to keep them nice and warm in winter but are, equally, very well ventilated. Good ventilation is essential to the health of the donkeys combined with the warmth that they

13

Sheep cropping the grass.

find so necessary, since they are not indigenous to the United Kingdom.

We have a number of sheep at the sanctuary; I bought six many years ago, because we were advised by our veterinary department that sheep cropping the grass are excellent in preventing parasitic infestation of the ground as they can eat and absorb most donkey parasite larvae without any ill-effects to themselves, and prove a very good method of keeping clean pastures. Since that early purchase and the acquisition of a Jacob ram, nature had taken its course and I was somewhat amused to see my flock of Jacob sheep who had been sheared the day before by John Rabjohns, our farm manager, looking very thin and different from the great shaggy creatures they had been two days before. The donkeys and sheep seem to get on very well together and we have never had any problems at all with keeping them; we transfer them regularly from field to field as they are required.

Early in the afternoon I returned to the sanctuary for a 2 p.m. meeting with Dr McGregor and Dr Swan who had asked if they could meet me to discuss the Slade Centre. They arrived right on time and proved to be a most charming couple. Both zoologists, they had been at Devon County Show when the children gave their displays and had been so impressed that they had decided to do something constructive to enable more children to have the advantages given to handicapped youngsters within a radius of the Slade Centre at Sidmouth. They had decided to club together and put up sufficient money to start a Slade Centre in the Leicester area where they live. It was a most encouraging and interesting afternoon's discussion; having been through the problems, both financial and practical, of building the Slade Centre from scratch I was able to give them sufficient information to either fire them with enthusiasm or dampen their spirits, depending on their state of mind. Fortunately for me, they were fired with enthusiasm and I became more and more encouraged as I realized that their thoughts were running completely parallel to mine and that they seemed to be aware of all the immense problems they could face, but were prepared to tackle the project and to keep it totally non-commercial. So many people who come to

Uncovering sores in the Ethiopian market.

see us with ideas either don't have the staying power, don't realize the cost involved or have an ulterior motive for suggesting either starting a sanctuary or a Slade Centre that we do sometimes get rather discouraged; but I was quite sure that here was a very genuine offer of help for children that we were unable to reach and I left the meeting extremely hopeful that, although it would not happen soon, in the long term a Slade Centre could be started in the Leicester area. I was able to offer suitable donkeys for the project and help and advice, not only in the building itself, but also in the day-to-day running of the centre with, of course, complete cost breakdowns which would be invaluable to them when assessing how much money they would need and appealing for funds.

The day I started school, shortly after my fifth birthday, I met a little girl on the doorstep called June Evers and, although it is now many years ago, we have remained firm friends ever since; after my husband left me June came to live with me, a wonderful solution for both of us. She is devoted to donkeys and animals and is the most wonderful help to me in every way. Generally on a Saturday we try to go out in the evening to make a break in the week but this Saturday she was involved, with me, in another problem indirectly caused by the sanctuary.

As you possibly know one of the other charities I run, the International Donkey Protection Trust, works abroad trying to help donkeys. On a recent visit to Ethiopia, where we hope to treat 3·5 million donkeys with anthelmintic (parasite dose), we had been working closely with the Addis Ababa Veterinary University which is situated in Debre Zeit, a

To handicapped children the gentle donkey is a source of wonderment.

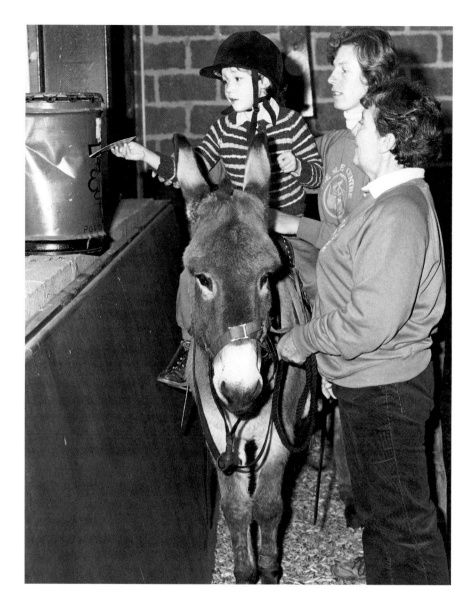

Posting a letter by 'donkey mail'.

small town some fifty miles from the capital itself. We had had a quite traumatic time there; four of us went—myself, June Evers, Charlie Courtney, a farm manager, and our vet Fiona Taylor. June and I had previously visited and had been appalled at the state of the donkeys in their big markets; many were covered in unpleasant sores and the general condition of the animals could only be described as poor. Considering that donkeys in Ethiopia are one of the most important agricultural assets, to improve the lot of the donkey so that it can do its work better and live longer would be a most practical way to help the Ethiopian people; with this in mind we hoped to make a real contribution to the country's problems. We had discussed carefully how to cope with the terrible saddle galls from which they suffer and Fiona Taylor, the vet, had come up with the brilliant idea of taking long strips of Tubigauze, stuffing them full of cotton wool and making sausage-like pads which could be put round the terrible sores to ease the pressure when the heavy burden was replaced on the donkey's back and we spent many hours of hard, dirty work in the markets doing just this job. The humans were often in a bad state too, and we had to treat many adults and children suffering from things such as leprosy, skin ulcers and scabies as it felt totally wrong to put a clean dressing on a donkey's back and ignore the sufferings of the child or person standing next to you.

Having finished our work in Ethiopia we were about to leave when one of the professors, Dr Aberra Ayana, suddenly pleaded with us to try to help in the case of a little girl called Meron Tsegaye whom he knew personally and who was going blind and deaf through what the hospital there described as increasing intracranial pressure. Up to a few days earlier the girl had been quite normal and it now appeared suddenly that she was fated at best to become blind and deaf and likely to lose her life through this sudden serious illness. He told us that the hospital in Addis Ababa said they were totally unable to help and her only hope was to go to some western country where they had more sophisticated equipment and could possibly stop the increase of the pressure or treat it in some way. I promised to do the best I could, so when I got back to England I had spent some time trying to get aid for this little girl but with very little success. A desperate telex from Addis Ababa forced me to make a decision and I decided that I would back the project myself and immediately bought a ticket for her and her aunt to come over to the UK and be admitted to hospital. I had to bring her aunt over because of Meron's age and the fact that she could speak no English, and what a wise decision it turned out to be.

Meron had been in Exeter hospital for some time and had just been transferred down to Plymouth where a neuro-surgeon was available and so Saturday night this week was to be spent down at the hospital. Another of the projects of the IDPT has been to bring Third World vets over to the UK and give them the opportunity to visit veterinary universities here and to spend four or five weeks studying our facilities and special skills in donkeys' needs so that they can go back to their own countries more able to help the donkeys there and, in fact, to be an excellent link for us with the veterinary departments in their particular countries. We had already invited Dr Yilma Makonnen from Ethiopia to visit and he had, in fact, come on the same flight as Meron and Senait, her aunt, and so we took Yilma down with us to Plymouth to visit Meron. It provided us with a very good chance to discuss his progress to date in England, after two weeks with us, and he certainly appeared to be getting a great deal out of the visit. He was looking forward to visiting the University of Glasgow Veterinary School the following week when he would have an opportunity to discuss problems in Ethiopia with well known veterinary parasitologists such as Dr Jimmy Duncan and Prof. Max Murray. Like us, he was extremely concerned at Meron's condition and we were pleased to find her reasonably cheerful in Freedom Fields hospital. On the way home, at 10.45 p.m., I popped into the sanctuary for a final visit to see there were no problems and was happy to find all was well. I was able to give Lucy and Katy a good-night pat; they looked much more settled although I noted that John had not yet done their feet to give them a bit more time to acclimatize. They were obviously much happier than they had been in the morning and I went to bed fairly satisfied with my day's work.

A view of the sanctuary fields.

SUN

DAY

Sunday started off as a beautiful day. I awoke to hear the happy brays of the donkeys galloping across the fields; it is a constant source of pleasure to me that from my house I can see and hear my donkeys day and night. I find them extremely intelligent animals and normally they don't bray unless there is a problem—possibly they are hungry, or a stallion happens to see a mare. If they do bray at night generally it is a fox crossing the field or some real problem, and our night watchmen know to walk around to investigate if there is any undue noise. However, this Sunday morning it was purely high spirits and I watched, fascinated, as a group of the nursery donkeys chased each other round the field with the most enormous energy and enthusiasm. Two of the young geldings managed to grab each other by their collars and began a game that many of the donkeys seem to enjoy, that is, seeing who could pull the collar off the other donkey's neck. We do have problems with identification particularly on our other farms where sometimes up to a hundred donkeys are running in one group. It's never very easy for the manager to walk into a field and find five identical looking brown donkeys, all collarless, with five collars lying around on the grass.

Having experienced many problems with this in the past, we have now got a small ankle bracelet on each donkey bearing its number but, yet again, this can occasionally cause problems, especially where donkeys are given access to woodland or more rough pasture where these can get caught up on small saplings or pieces of wood. We were most delighted to be given a demonstration this week of a very tiny microchip which has been developed and which can be inserted painlessly into the crest of the donkey's neck. Once there, it is a permanent fixture and by simply running a small camera-like hand-held piece of equipment over the donkey's neck a digital number is displayed, individual to that donkey, to provide a permanent marking system. This

system has taken many years to develop and, in fact, has only just been perfected to the stage where we feel we can try it on fifty of our donkeys. Both my vets are extremely pleased with the results to date and certainly the donkeys never even seem to feel the small injection needed to place this microchip in their necks. It certainly solves, permanently, the problem of identification, particularly in case the donkeys are ever stolen or get lost from a rehabilitation home, as we now have over 960 donkeys out in good homes. However, the two young donkeys playing that morning were very well known to me indeed and there would be no problem in identifying them if they happened to pull each other's collars off.

Although I was down on the yards early, John Fowler was already doing Katy's feet, having found both donkeys in a much better state of mind and health on the Sunday morning. The other donkeys were happily enjoying their breakfasts and all seemed very quiet as I took off the ansaphone messages and dealt with the queries from the night watchman. Amongst the ansaphone messages was an urgent call with regard to two thin-looking donkeys with very long feet which two ladies had apparently seen whilst on a canal barge trip in the Midlands. The details of the exact location of the donkeys were extremely sparse and, having rung Roy Harrington, our senior inspector, and passed the message over to him, I left him the problem of trying to get the local inspector for the area to find the donkeys as soon as possible. The details which we are given of donkeys in trouble can sometimes be very vague; people on the telephone say, 'I was on a train between X and Y and looking out through the window about four fields away saw this donkey lying down that I think was in trouble, can your inspectors go and visit it?' I must give all credit to my inspectors, they almost always find the animal in trouble. This particular Sunday morning as I went back up home, I couldn't help chuckling at the thought of the

'I've got your collar.'

poor inspector renting a barge and touring around the canals of the Midlands.

June and I, having had dogs all our lives, both had a similar misfortune of losing our dogs some seven months ago from old age. Living together as we were, we decided we'd love to have a few dogs and June, who had just taken early retirement from her life-long job as superintendent of radiography, decided she would like to show and breed dogs as a hobby and so we had bought two standard poodles and two toy poodles as puppies. Taking the dogs on my Sunday morning rounds, this particular day, I was going to walk the new land we had purchased adjoining the sanctuary.

This 86 acres became available just as we were contemplating a move to Norfolk. We had been advised that the donkeys would appreciate the lower rainfall in cold weather in Norfolk, and would be able to exercise a lot more in the fields during winter than here, where it is rather damp and cold. Donkeys hate

(Left) *Typical Devon bank.*

(Right) *Donkeys like their shelters.*

rain and cold combined, although it has always been thought that cold on its own was no deterrent to their enjoying an outside life. However, the move to Norfolk had been delayed because we had found during the previous two years when Devon had had exceptionally cold dry spells that our donkeys, instead of taking medical advice and galloping out in the fields in the cold weather, had definitely decided they preferred the warmth of their infra-red lamps and their large airy barns. So we were having second thoughts about the project of opening a large sanctuary for approximately a thousand donkeys in East Anglia. This land came up just at the time when we were trying to make a decision and seemed heaven sent. We have, of course, many fantastic facilities here, the hospital, the isolation blocks, all the medical facilities needed and extra care boxes for the many intake cases arriving;

another 86 acres adjoining our land so that we could make use of these facilities seemed too good to miss. The Trustees agreed with Brian and my proposals and the land had been bought. Having once managed to raise the finance to buy land our problems always just seemed to be starting.

Donkeys love foraging in banks and eating the bark from trees and I must say I am very fond indeed of Devon banks and we have always managed to fence far enough away so that the donkeys are not able to eat the wild plants and flowers or damage the bank itself. The new land we had purchased had already had many of its banks taken out and the fields had become rather too large for our special method of grazing. Donkeys can very quickly overgraze a pasture and good management means giving fields ample time to rest in between the grazing and so we decided that we would reinstate the Devon banks that had been pulled down to make the fields a suitable size for the donkeys. We also had to make shelters for the donkeys because, even in the summer, they need somewhere to get out of the sun and away from the flies and, of course, the rain, which, in Devon we can suffer during the supposed summer months. I also decided it would be a good idea to make a really nice walk around the whole property so that visitors could wander around all the fields and enjoy watching the donkeys without having the opportunity to leave any gates open or disturb them in any way. Having worked it out very carefully, we designed a walk of almost two and a half miles; we would have had to fence every hedge in any event and it cost no more to make the walk than to make the fields secure for the donkeys. It was at this stage that, to our great delight, we were left a bequest in the will of a life-long donkey supporter and a request that the money she left should be used to enhance the beauty of the sanctuary and its surroundings and for the benefit of the donkeys. It was decided that we would plant an avenue of trees around the walk which would act as a wind protector and sun shield for the donkeys as well as giving enjoyment to the many visitors who would come through the area.

On this Sunday morning June and I, and our dogs, walked around to check how everything was getting on. The walk was now beginning to look like a walk and the trees were already in situ and doing well. We stopped for some time at the new barns that were being erected. The cost of the whole project had escalated in view of its size; we had now managed to put up the main frame and structure of the buildings but the last bit, which included the concreting out of the bottom and the building of walls to meet the Yorkshire boarding halfway up, seemed an insurmountable amount to raise. I was very

'The walk was beginning to look like a walk.'

One of the new barns.

worried as we stood there because I suddenly realized that our escalating expenses on the day-to-day running of the charity were going to eat up too many of our funds to complete the buildings in time for this summer. I decided I must have a long talk with Brian on Monday to see what suggestions he had as to how we could best cope with the problem.

Having dropped the dogs back home I walked down to the sanctuary to find the yard absolutely full of visitors. Sunday is the busiest day of the week and we have become a very popular tourist venue. I have always felt that as we are a registered charity anybody who donates money has a right to see how it is being used and therefore have never made any charge whatsoever for admission, either for people or cars, to people visiting. It now seems that many people visit Sidmouth and the surrounding

areas with the prime object of coming up to see the sanctuary and Sundays have become so busy that I have to have two staff on just for what we call 'show-around'. Both were very busy on this Sunday, there were most interesting things for people to see and our new foal was causing a great attraction as was, of course, Blackie, the donkey we had rescued from Spain.

One of the objects of the Donkey Sanctuary is to educate children as far as possible to prevent further cases of cruelty to donkeys happening in the future and to this end we have prepared a 'Lesson on the Donkey' which is sent free to every school in the UK. We also get thousands of children visiting us during the year and this day was no exception, with two coaches of youngsters coming in, making a total of over ninety in one go. Suddenly the yards were full of bustling, excited children, the

Sunday visitors start arriving.

donkeys standing watching and enjoying all the extra fuss that they received. In our information room we have a video set and during the day we play the various films and videos that have been taken at the sanctuary so that people have the advantage of seeing the other four farms from the comfort of a chair. We also sell a few selected items, all produced by ourselves, and all, of course, to do with donkeys. Many people have asked us to sell things like pens, car-stickers and diaries, the list is endless, but I have always felt that the money we receive should be used directly for the donkeys' needs and not tied up in large stocks of goods to be sold. If a commercial firm was providing us with the goods then, obviously, their job would be to make a profit and the donkeys would have to pay for this. People come from all round the world to visit the Donkey Sanctuary, it is amazing that people, even from New Zealand, Australia and Canada, have all heard about us and make a point of visiting.

We get some amusing incidents where complete strangers will walk up to me in the yard and say, 'Oh, Mrs Svendsen, you know me well because I've seen you on TV,' and they find it quite difficult to understand that I cannot remember them—having never even set eyes on them.

Our hens and donkeys like to see the latest information.

M O N

DAY

Monday morning started very early indeed, to be exact at 3.30 a.m. The previous November we had had a call from an extremely concerned lady who had bought what she described as a run-down farm, with the intention of starting it up as equine stables. Having moved in and taken stock of her new surroundings, she was highly surprised to find two small, white donkeys left abandoned in one of the fields. One was very obviously a stallion and the other, unfortunately, the stallion's mother. Both had very bad feet and, according to the new owner, did not look in terribly good condition. The new owner telephoned the sanctuary to ask if we could possibly help and our inspector immediately went down to see what could be done. Our inspector was very concerned: she had had her eye on these donkeys for two years and during that time had tried to persuade the previous owner to part with them as she realized that the son, called Just William, was an entire stallion and was quite capable of serving his mother. However, the owner had steadfastly refused to have the colt castrated, repeating that she was going to find a good home for them. So the two little donkeys, Just William and his mother Jenny, arrived into our care on November 24th last year.

Our veterinary surgeon aged Jenny at about sixteen years old and her son as a two-year-old and it was quite apparent that Jenny was already in foal. As we didn't want to split the two donkeys, they stayed together for two or three days until they had settled down and then both together were quietly led to the hospital entrance. Here Just William was given a small shot of anaesthetic and, with Jenny watching, laid down quietly on the specially designed pads which are used for transporting the donkeys into our hospital theatre. At this stage Jenny was led out and put into the recovery box where Just William would be returning in a short while, no longer a stallion. After his operation Just William came round to find his mother next to him and within a few hours both were peacefully feeding again with the absolute minimum of trauma experienced by either. We are always very, very careful when treating donkeys for any illness or routine surgery to keep the stress minimal and within a few days both were happily together back in the isolation block. During the six-week isolation period that all donkeys undergo when they arrive they are given intensive care from head to foot, inoculated against equine flu and tetanus, and given a complete medical examination. Their diet and needs are carefully assessed over the six-week period before they are allocated to one of our farms. Jenny and Just William were sent to Brookfield Farm, which is just four miles away; there fit, healthy donkeys are able to live the sort of life they enjoy most: that is, regular feeding, grooming, large airy barns and yards to run out in and, of course, the sight of the beautiful grass they will be able to enjoy once the summer has come and the rains have receded.

In view of her impending foaling a very close eye was kept on Jenny and Just William and, some three weeks ago, they had been brought back to Slade House Farm together so that we could keep an eye on them during the short time before the foaling was expected. It is always extremely difficult to tell when a donkey is about to foal, the gestation period can be from 11 to 13 months so, even if one knows the date of service, a specified time for the new arrival cannot be counted on. Here, however, we had another problem in that we had no idea when Just William had served his mother. As this was an in-breeding case we felt Jenny should be near the best possible medical help. The night watchman going on his rounds had noticed Just William standing outside the box at 3 a.m. and had thought it rather unusual as there was a light drizzle of rain. However, he had looked closely at Jenny and could see no problem at all.

Just William.

Obviously Jenny had timed the watchman carefully because it must have been shortly after he had passed on his rounds that quietly and with no fuss at all a little colt foal arrived.

Within minutes of his phone call, I was in the stable looking at the new foal. Rather surprisingly the foal was grey, as both parents were completely white and we had thought that perhaps we could expect a different colour to the general donkey grey. However, the main thing was that the little chap was in fine fettle and in no time at all was gambolling around the stable as if to the manner born. Things didn't seem quite so good for Just William or indeed for any of the veterinary staff or myself going in to have a look at Jenny. She decided this was definitely her foal and nobody, human or animal, was going to get near it except her, and so we carefully left her as she was being such a good mother and there was no point in any intervention. It was certainly a happy start to a Monday morning and, although we hadn't named the foal at that time, as soon as I told my secretary, Mal, of the new arrival she reminded me of the letter we had received very recently from the secretary of a firm of London solicitors, Mrs Sullivan. This letter had come in response to a circular campaign we did to businesses and firms throughout the United Kingdom.

In April this year the law was changed with regard to charitable giving and for the first time, provided a firm put in a scheme which was approved by the government, employees could actually give money to charity before that money was taxed; in the past, income had to be taxed before any donations to charity were made. This new method would enable the firm to deduct up to £150 a year from an employee's salary before it was rated for tax, this then to be sent to one of the approved charitable collection centres where it would then be sent on to the nominated charity. Many very large companies in this country have been running charity schemes for years but, of course, never

with untaxed income. So we felt it was a good idea that the employees of companies were made fully aware of the Donkey Sanctuary, the Slade Centre and the International Donkey Protection Trust so that they could nominate our charity to their employers. We sent the circular out to 75,000 companies and had the most amazing response. Many companies, as requested, put the poster up on their notice boards, but, of course, it is too early to gauge the results of this yet as the scheme is only just getting into operation. A bonus, however, was the enormous number of individuals who decided, regardless of the payroll giving scheme, to send us a donation and this had been the case with the following delightful letter from Mrs Sullivan:

11 Stone Buildings
Lincoln's Inn
London

Dear Madam,
In March you sent to my firm, Edwin Coe &
Calder Woods, some information about your
Donkey Sanctuary. As I open the post at this
solicitor's office I was interested in your poster,
having a great love of donkeys. I came up with
an idea to get some funds for these beautiful
animals. Whereas a lot of the secretaries would
donate something to an animal charity, I
wanted the solicitors to participate as well and
to get them to part with their money!
I hit on the idea of cooking and taking it to
work to sell. I started with toffee; it sold well,
but I found most ladies were on diets—so then
came up with quiche lorraine. That was the best
idea which went very well. It's not something I
could do on a regular basis, getting it to work is
rather awkward as I have to travel quite a
distance on several forms of transport. I always
say people know I have something fragile as
they always knock into me.

Donkeys are almost always inquisitive.

However, from the sale of my produce and donations from some of the staff I have collected £21·31 which I am sending to you for the donkeys. I am pleased that you are doing something for these poor creatures. When I can do some more cooking you will get the proceeds. Please find cheque enclosed.

Do you ever name any donkey that comes to you without a name? If so, is it possible to name one Lincoln? We work in Lincoln's Inn, so it would be nice if we could have a donkey named Lincoln, we could donate cash from time to time and it would help me 'sell' if I could say he's named after our work location. Also, do you have any money boxes with the Sanctuary name on. We use an envelope at the moment but a box would be a better advert.

Finally, my husband and I (he helps with the cooking, he also loves donkeys—a combined effort you could say) are so happy there is a Sanctuary for these beasts to find peace and tranquillity in the twilight of their years. Keep up the good work; I will try to keep donations coming to you. If you do name a donkey is it possible to have a colour photo to stick on our wall?

Yours faithfully,

Mrs S. Sullivan

With regard to her request about naming a baby donkey, we decided that Jenny and Just William's son should be called Lincoln.

Having checked up first thing in the morning to make sure that mother, father and foal were all doing well, we settled into the normal Monday routine.

There is always a great deal of mail on a Monday morning. I sort out Saturday's when it comes but, of course, it has to wait until Monday to be activated. Amongst the letters was one from the World Society for the Protection of Animals of which we are members. About three years ago there had been a big article in the American press about mules being

Lincoln's first day out.

made to jump from enormous heights into large containers full of water in New Jersey, New York and Florida. This was a sort of circus act and the people running the act stated categorically that the mules thoroughly enjoyed this and did it voluntarily. Neither the WSPA or myself had agreed with this and on my visit to America to try to solve the problem of the donkeys being shot in Death Valley some three years previously I had been assured that this circus act no longer took place in America. However, in a recent magazine it had been stated that this had all started again and I had been extremely concerned, so had written to WSPA. Their letter stated quite categorically that this was still going on and had now moved to Europe, but they did not name specific areas where it was happening. These reports, uncertified by dates and times and places, are always difficult to follow up. This type of cruelty is extremely emotive but very often by the time the report is published the problem has been tackled and dealt with; nevertheless, one of my first letters that morning was to our various contacts throughout Europe to try to find out if anyone could give me any information on this horrific practice.

Everything else seemed to be running smoothly that morning. John Rabjohns, the farm manager, came in and reported that all was well; he had men erecting fences up on the new land and the new method of grazing, using the electric fencing, was working well. The problems with turning donkeys out to grass are that some of them tend to eat far too much, and that they are extremely selective grazers: if we give them a whole field at a time we find that some of the grass becomes foul before they can eat it, and some donkeys just eat and eat and eat and never stop. Our new methods, which can be used because we have such extensive fields, mean that the fence is moved a few feet further

Eeyore, Frosty and Pancho in their grazing area (you can just see the electric fence).

each day giving the donkeys a fresh daily bite. All the donkeys in intensive care and isolation seemed fine and Pat Feather had been in to report that all was well at Slade although she was expecting a particularly busy day as a new class was coming from one of the regular schools. This meant quite a lot of extra work for Pat and her team of helpers. The children who come regularly know exactly what to expect at the centre: there is a spacious play area as well as the donkeys, which they can pet and love and have a ride on. To handicapped children, especially those with mental handicaps, even the change of environment can be quite traumatic and so a new group means a lot more hard work and patience for the morning ride. It is quite amazing how some of the children who arrive totally hyperactive settle down when they see the gentle, placid donkeys and how almost every child automatically reaches out to touch the donkeys and relate to them in a most charming manner. I promised Pat I would try to slip over to Slade to see how things were going later in the morning. I had a rather important job to do that Monday morning as, over the last few weeks, quite a few beautiful items of jewellery had been sent in to us by subscribers to be sold so that the funds could go to the donkeys.

To anyone who has had the job of selling jewellery such as rings, brooches and earrings it will be no surprise to hear that this can be quite difficult. I think we always tend to put rather more value on our possessions than other people do and some of our subscribers, sending in items precious beyond words to them, would be very disappointed were we not to raise the maximum possible from each single item. I had taken this particular set of jewellery to Exeter the previous week but had not felt like leaving any as the prices offered were so low. Amongst the items were about seven which had formed part of a legacy left to us earlier in the year. The solicitors had obtained a probate value and asked our permission to sell them, but having

looked through the list I did feel it was rather low and we opted instead to take the jewellery to see if I could get more for it. The amount offered by the dealer in Exeter had, in fact, been less than the actual probate value for the items in question which gave me a very good idea of the sort of prices I was being given. Fortunately, I have always been very interested in antiques and there was no way I was going to let these go below the value I anticipated. I had another dealer in mind, and this morning I slipped out with my precious bundle to see if I could do any better than the week before in Exeter.

As the dealer looked at the rings and jewels I must say I felt a very strange and rather sad feeling. So many had obviously been very precious to these people and I knew I had to do my utmost to get the best money possible for the donkeys which was, or indeed would have been, their wish. I offered first the small group that had been in the probate and it took over half an hour of haggling before we agreed on a figure which was almost 50% more than that of the probate value. Heartened by this, I was able to go ahead with the other jewellery knowing that I had, at least, an honest dealer and came back to the sanctuary extremely pleased with a cheque for £1,100 in my bag—a most useful addition to our funds.

Although this money would be nowhere near enough to complete the barns we so desperately needed, it at least gave us a hand, and we had had a marvellous donation a short time before from a lady in Blackpool which had in fact covered the whole cost of one barn so at least we knew we could cope during the coming winter. Raising funds for our enormous (and growing) number of donkeys is a constant nightmare as 3,060 donkeys take a lot of keep and feed; there are also the wages and salaries for 92 full-time staff, each one doing an essential job in maintaining the high standards of the charity. Brian and I discussed that

Individual grooming—an essential job.

morning ways of meeting our financial requirements.

Donkeys need a great deal of individual care and attention and skilled handling and, whilst we use volunteers wherever possible, we have found that with volunteers there is a lack of continuity which can adversely affect the donkeys' welfare. Despite the cost of the staff we still manage to keep our administration costs down to only 4p in the £1, these figures being supplied by the Charities Aid Foundation who do a completely independent assessment of all the top charities in the UK. I am always most anxious to see the figures when published, to make quite sure that we are still staying on the same lines, and that the money is going where we all want it to go—to the donkeys and nowhere else. Our newsletter which now goes out to nearly 70,000 subscribers twice a year usually brings in a marvellous response. People like to be kept informed of what's going on at the sanctuary and how their favourite donkeys are progressing. We also rely heavily on legacies, and take great pride in feeling that the money left by people is used as they would have wished and that their contribution has really helped in keeping us going. Our Memory Wall is very popular; the name of everybody who leaves money to the sanctuary is engraved on large plaques and we feel this is a nice way to immortalize those who have helped us in no matter how small a way.

After lunch Neil Harvey, who looks after the isolation group, came to me with a problem about two little donkeys, both overweight, who had been in an extremely good home until their owner's circumstances had changed; they were absolutely refusing to eat anything put in front of them. John Fowler, our senior vet, Neil and myself were all very concerned as donkeys, particularly from good homes, tend to be at greater risk than those from poor homes. What happens is that the donkey has become very overweight and petted at home, and if it refuses to eat because it's so distressed to lose its own

Carrot rations—just like home!

home and family and its familiar tit-bits, it can begin to lose weight too drastically. This sets up a state known as hyperlipaemia which can end in death. In losing weight the fat particles begin to disintegrate and these are then carried away in the blood system. If this progresses too fast it becomes irreversible and the blood system can become completely clogged by the fatty particles, causing death. When we take in donkeys who have had the misfortune to lose very good homes it is a constant problem to stop this happening and, quite rightly, Neil brought it to my attention. We were, luckily, able to solve this one as we found that the two donkeys absolutely loved chopped-up carrots and apples; this, obviously, had been part of their previous diet and it was very rewarding that afternoon to see them eating their bowl of bran almost concealed among the chopped-up apples and carrots. We do try to treat every donkey as an individual despite the large numbers coming in and this is why our special, caring staff are so vitally important.

My last job of the day was to do a little more work on the lecture I was trying to prepare for Montreal. Every second year the World Association for the Advancement of Veterinary Parasitology holds a world congress; last time it was held in Rio de Janeiro and this year it will be in Montreal. Every fourth year the World Veterinary Association holds its big congress and the two tend to merge together. I had been asked to the meeting in Rio to give a paper on our work throughout the world on parasites in the donkey. Not without many misgivings, I had been to Rio and had an extremely good reception, so good in fact that the American Veterinary Parasitology Association had asked me to lecture in Atlanta last year which also met with enormous enthusiasm and now I have to give a lecture in Montreal. Over two thousand veterinarians from all round the world attend this congress and it is an absolutely nerve-racking experience to lecture to such knowledgeable people and it takes a considerable amount of time. One has to present the outline of the paper some six months before and then, of course, you can finalize it and get all your slides together a little nearer the time. In view of some of the difficult slides which I have to have made covering the more technical aspects of the talk I have to get this prepared in good time and the latter part of the afternoon was spent on this project. Montreal will be coming up in August and I just hope I have it ready in time.

Every donkey loves a good roll.

TUES

SDAY

Tuesday morning and disaster! I came down onto the yards at 7.45 a.m. to find that one of our dear old friends Bridget C. had died during the night. Bridget had come to the sanctuary in December 1982 and was forty when she arrived. She came with a great friend called Milly, from Yorkshire, and they had had quite a large number of health problems when they came in. Milly had suffered badly from laminitis and both donkeys had had lungworm which they appeared to have passed on to their owners' horses. Even five years ago the passing of lungworm from donkeys to horses was a common occurrence. Donkeys can have lungworm with no apparent ill-effects whatsoever, but a horse contracting it will immediately show bad symptoms of coughing and loss of wind and in 1982 when these donkeys came in it was a difficult problem to solve. Now, however, thanks to new drugs on the market it is perfectly possible to keep donkeys and horses together absolutely safely as the lungworm in the donkey can be totally controlled. Unfortunately, Milly had died two years after coming in and so Bridget had made new friends with a group of the geriatrics. We always know our group of oldies, who live in the main yard and have every special facility possible, are at risk purely because of their age, and Bridget was forty-five. However, there had been no signs whatsoever that she was in any sort of trouble and I always hate losing old friends. She had been fine at 7.30 the evening before but had been found dead at 9.20. Fiona Taylor, our second vet, set off to do a post-mortem examination although we were almost sure that her death was due to completely natural causes.

There was also another problem to sort out before the day's work could begin and that concerned poor old Just William. You will remember that he had become a father the day before and that at the time of the birth Jenny had not wanted him anywhere near. During the night, however, this had become even worse and poor Just William, if he walked anywhere near the stable door, was being kicked unmercifully. As it was pouring with rain outside the night watchman decided, wisely, to take him down into the yard group for the night so that, at least, he could get under shelter and, if necessary, start making new friends as it seemed his mother/wife had now turned her back on him permanently. As a temporary measure Just William had been put in the big barn with the oldies, who are a very gentle, caring group, but it seemed he had not enjoyed his evening there at all; possibly he had been upset by Bridget dying but it was a very unhappy little Just William who met me early in the morning. We all discussed what could be done for him and decided, in the end, to put him with a group of younger donkeys out in one of the fields and so the last I saw of him, before going into the office, was him trotting happily up the drive with one of the staff and going to join Buffalo's group with all the beach donkeys. Hopefully he would be able to settle down with this group which is mainly male geldings and included some youngsters as well who could be companions to him. Jenny had now settled down a lot and allowed me to come in and talk to her new little foal, Lincoln; her possessiveness seemed to be receding. She is, however, a very possessive mother and I was very careful to pay equal attention to her and not appear to make too much fuss of Lincoln. The night staff advised me that so long as Just William hadn't come near the door she had seemed perfectly contented. I spent an enjoyable five minutes watching Lincoln take his first faltering steps outside. I always love to see foals feeling grass under their hooves; they lift their little hooves up in surprise and then manage a hop, skip and jump just to show that they can cope with the new environment. Jenny kept a very close eye on him and he was only allowed to play out for a few minutes before she firmly nudged him back into the shelter of the foaling box with its warm infra-red lamp.

Just William playing with his new friend.

That morning was scheduled for managers' meeting. We have five farms and this means that some of the managers are out of contact with the events taking place around the main sanctuary. We therefore have regular meetings which include the veterinary staff as well where everybody can put their points of view and any problems can be thrashed out jointly. Over the years most policies relating to the management of the farms and the running of them have been thrashed out for each farm and now everybody knows the routines for getting the best out of the land for the donkeys. At this time of the year, it's getting near to the making of hayage

and also haymaking and all the managers had been asked to assess how many bales they were going to make this year so that, if we had to buy any hay for the remainder of the year, we could buy it 'off the field' at this stage at a better price than if we had to buy it in February or March of next year when the price would have escalated. I have great faith in all my managers; each one runs his own farm and we try to let them be reasonably independent within the general management guidelines on which we have all agreed. Whilst they don't find it easy to accurately forecast how many bales they are going to make from each field, equally, we

Hay-making.

*Voluntary help is
always welcome.*

administrators don't find it very easy to work out how many donkeys might come in over the next twelve months and what our actual feed requirements are going to be, so it is always quite a lively discussion.

This year we have, of course, an enormous advantage in the new land that we have bought. As the fencing is not quite completed no donkeys have been on the land yet which means that over two-thirds of it will be able to be turned into hay. At the end of the meeting it became apparent to me that, for the first time, this year we were not going to need to buy in any hay whatsoever—an enormous saving for us and much better for the donkeys. When we seed our land, we seed it with a special selection of grasses which the donkeys like and we are extremely careful to make sure that ragwort and other poisonous weeds are eradicated before we make hay so that there is no danger of poisonous hay being produced. When we have to buy our hay in we insist on bales being broken open at random so that we can check and make sure there is no must or fustiness in the hay as this causes lung problems in donkeys. It can easily be caused by the hay being left on the field, or allowed to get wet, before it is stored in a dry barn. We also check that it smells sweet and fresh and, as far as we know, is clear from poisonous weeds. This year there will be no such problem as all our own hay will be stored as it is made, kept dry, and will provide excellent fodder for the following year.

One of our farms, Town Barton, has an added facility which was put in two years ago. Many of the donkeys with breathing problems are much better if they eat soaked grass or a type of silage which we call hayage. This means the grass is partially allowed to dry and is then vacuum-packed to stop any moulds or viruses appearing in it; the donkeys can then eat this, finding it most palatable, without any risk of dust which affects the lung. Hayage is allowed to dry rather more than the normal silage, and is then stored in large towers at Town Barton

Farm. This method has been used down there for two years now and the donkeys seem to enjoy the food and we appear to get less lung and breathing problems. Our main problem is that many of these donkeys have come from poor homes and have been subjected to earlier problems of both feeding and management of which we are not aware. Some have had their lungs permanently damaged by not being treated for lungworm, others have gone through periods when they have not had the correct food and have suffered long-term internal damage. They may apparently arrive reasonably fit at the sanctuary, because some symptoms do not appear until many years later; then, as the donkeys go into old age, we find them suddenly developing lung problems, and in some cases these could have been lying dormant for many years.

We constantly strive to improve both our feeding and housing methods to the donkeys' benefit and a large amount of time at managers' meetings is usually spent discussing the problems of providing the maximum ventilation which the veterinary department would like to see imposed, tempered by the warmth and comfort felt necessary by the managers for the general well-being of the donkeys. As administrators, our job is to strike the happy medium and to ensure that the donkeys get the best deal possible for them. Managers' meetings always end with lunch, generally up at my house, so that everybody can relax a little and have a good chat. The managers then spend the afternoon around Slade House Farm bringing themselves up to date with the events that have taken place since the last meeting and perhaps offering helpful suggestions with regard to donkeys whom they have had for many years but who have now become geriatric and come back into the special care given at Slade House Farm. Everybody makes great friends with certain donkeys and we all keep these long-term friendships going. It's quite amazing how the donkeys will remember the voices and the

touch of those they have known and who have known them many years ago.

Today after lunch we had a large group of Bicton students who came from the Agricultural College. We have very close contact with the college and they sent a group of students on this occasion to watch John Fowler operating. On this particular day he was castrating one of our young colts that had been born at the sanctuary. Although this colt was only six months old he had already developed stallion tendencies and had been observed a few days earlier trying to ride his mother. Obviously the name I had given him of Rambo seemed to fit! The operation was so successful that within a few hours Rambo was up and trotting around again and within two days he and his mother had rejoined their group. The students also spent some time in the laboratory where we are running haematology trials to establish a norm for the donkeys' blood count. They also had an opportunity to chat to Yilma, the Ethiopian vet, and the hospital and yard seemed absolutely full of white-coated students. I was recalled to the office just before 4 p.m. to find the veterinary surgeon from Cyprus ringing to confirm my arrival time in Cyprus next week.

Trips abroad have to be planned a long time in advance, and on this occasion I had suddenly realized I just wouldn't be able to do the first leg, which was Greece, as work at the sanctuary had built up so heavily over the last few days. This meant that the next tour would start in Cyprus. Dr George Evstathiou was one of the vets proposed by the World Health Organization who had visited us last year on the scheme we had set up, similar to that of Dr Yilma. Following this he was now prepared to set up a trial for which we had worked out a protocol in Cyprus and my job was to meet the government and vets and make sure that there were no problems in the areas they had chosen for the trial and in the selection of the donkeys. The marvellous news in Cyprus had been that we

(Left) *Lamu donkeys foraging for food on the rubbish dump.*

(Right) *Work starts on the Lamu sanctuary.*

(Below) *The new sanctuary's covered yard; it has a water trough available for donkeys inside and on the waterfront.*

had offered to pay for the anthelmintic to treat the donkeys but Dr George had phoned to tell me that the government had now decided they would put up all the money to dose the 9,800 donkeys in Cyprus. This was certainly a marvellous way to start a tour and I was as happy as Dr George at the news.

The next leg to Egypt would be a lot more difficult but, once again, I would have the big advantage of dealing with Dr Ragheb who had also visited us under our scheme and he himself was extremely keen to get the project going. Our last trip to Egypt had been rather disastrous as we were not entirely welcomed by the local population. It was the only place we have worked where we felt slightly unwelcome. Probably because we were white, possibly because we were women; whatever the reason, it was the only place in the world where both June and I had felt completely out of place. We had been working with the Brooke Hospital, which is an extremely good charity in Egypt, along with their 'dressers', who did a magnificent job putting dressings on the many wounds found on Egyptian donkeys. Under the circumstances we decided not to go back to Egypt but to support the Brooke Hospital practically by giving funds and, up to now, we had not seen an opportunity to return. However, Dr Ragheb had expressed great interest in anthelmintics for the donkeys in Egypt and any chance to improve their lot was worth taking, so the next port of call, after Cyprus, was to be Cairo and following on from that would be a return to Kenya.

The International Donkey Protection Trust has been working there for two years and on my last visit I was able to complete the purchase of a building absolutely ideal for the donkeys' needs on the island of Lamu, north-east of Mombasa. The donkeys in this area had been in desperate need when we first arrived. Being an island there is absolutely no other transport but donkeys; the streets are between four and six feet wide and, therefore, no vehicles will ever be able to be used. Donkeys carry everything from consumer goods to building materials, including large mahogany planks coming off the docks. All water on the island has to be drawn up from wells and normally the donkeys, if they were lucky, were only watered late at night when their work was finished and many times our team had watched donkeys desperate with thirst having to drink sea water with the most disastrous results; one of the intentions of the new sanctuary premises was to provide a drinking trough for the donkeys. The position of the property is such that almost every donkey working in Lamu walks past its walls and so a large drinking trough placed in the wall and kept filled would provide immediate help for the majority of donkeys in the area. Another problem is lack of food. Many of the people are in great distress themselves and buying food for their donkey is just not possible. There is some grazing at the back of the island during and after the rainy season but there are times when this becomes almost non-existent. At these times the donkeys tend to be turned away when work is finished and they have to forage through the refuse dumps and rubbish tips around the town to gain the necessary sustenance.

The sanctuary, hopefully, will hold a feeding clinic each night when those donkeys turned away and starving can, in fact, be fed. Another advantage is that we are right next door to the Veterinary Department of the Ministry and two vets are in constant attendance there and they have expressed their willingness to treat the donkeys for a very small fee indeed. A marvellous young man called Abdalla, whom I met on my first trip to Lamu and who has been working with me ever since will be the manager and I am quite convinced that the daily care that will now be able to be given to these donkeys will make an immense difference to their lives.

My trip on this occasion is to officially open the new sanctuary and we have invited local dignitaries and friends who have helped make the purchase possible. The previous owner of the property is Dr Fagin who lives on the island, having fallen in love with it on a visit many years ago. A retired specialist, he now lives an idyllic life out there, walking miles every day and really enjoying his retirement. When I approached him to purchase the property he seemed an extremely hard and tough business-man; he pointed out he had retired many years ago and he had to augment his income occasionally by selling properties. He already had somebody else interested in the property, which I knew was ideal for the donkeys, and I felt myself lucky to be able to purchase it at the price I did, after a great deal of bargaining. Having completed our deal on my last trip we both shook hands and he came around in the evening to finalize the deal which we were both put to our lawyers. At the end of our meeting I passed him my autobiography *Down Among the Donkeys*, which he said he would read.

The following morning I met him on the little narrow street in Lamu while walking up towards our proposed new property and, to my surprise, he rushed straight across to me and put his arms around me.

'Mrs Svendsen,' he said, 'I sat up the whole night reading your book and I really have the greatest admiration for you and all the work that you are doing. I realized I don't really need all the money that I've got and I would like to take £3,000 off the price that we both agreed as a contribution towards your charity,' and with that we both burst into tears as we stood on that hot little street in Lamu. Dr Fagin will be an honoured guest at the opening which we hope will be by the District Commissioner or Mr A. Otham, Chief of Lamu. The date will be July 4th, 1987, Independence Day for the donkeys in Lamu.

———————●———————

Donkeys lying in the sunshine.

WEDN

ESDAY

Wednesday morning and a little donkey called Kenny was due to have an operation to remove sarcoids. Kenny and his friend, Emma's Boy, had both come in together last July as young colts from a very caring but elderly owner who, unfortunately, found that at her age coping with eight donkeys was quite a handful, particularly because the other six were fillies and the two little boys were beginning to get ideas. Of course they both had to be gelded on their arrival but had had no problems with this and had settled down happily together. Unfortunately, Kenny had been afflicted with the most terrible growths, which we call sarcoids, in various places on his body. These seem to be a problem with many donkeys; some of the sarcoids are benign but, occasionally, we get one which turns cancerous and our vets have spent a great deal of time in perfecting treatment which is suitable either to eliminate them completely or, if this is not possible, at least to control them.

Kenny, now almost two, was due to have four sarcoids removed that particular morning. By far the worst was a great big one on the base of his left ear and the new cryosurgery treatment which means, literally, deep freezing the base of the growth, was going to be used here once he was anaesthetized. We have now found that by using this, together with a BCG vaccine on tumours reduced by diathermy, a sort of electrical current, we can cure many of the sarcoids and this method was used on the poor little donkey. Emma's Boy, his friend, waited patiently while Kenny was in the hospital and was delighted to see his friend return after he had recovered from his anaesthetic and treatment. In total four sarcoids had been dealt with and Fiona, the vet, was extremely hopeful that this would solve the problem.

Next on the operating table was Trixie. This little donkey had arrived in September 1982 and her condition on the admission sheet was reported as 'Thin and hungry, covered in lice, has dermatitis and matted coat.' Despite the

intensive care Trixie had received over the years she developed a tumour on her fetlock which had already been successfully removed. Unfortunately, a new tumour had been discovered in her mouth which was growing rapidly and which had worried all of us considerably. Today a biopsy was carried out and the sample was to be sent to Bloxham Laboratories to see if

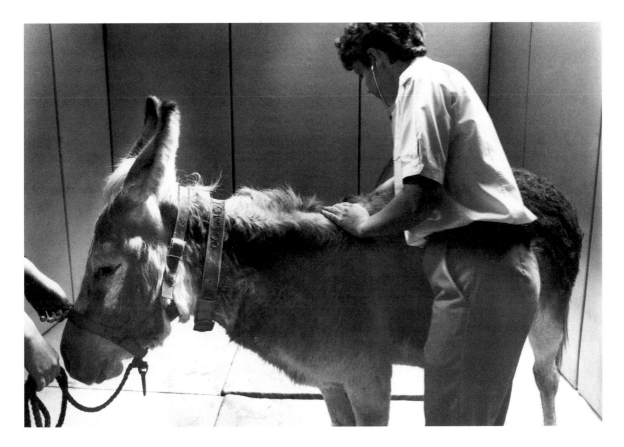

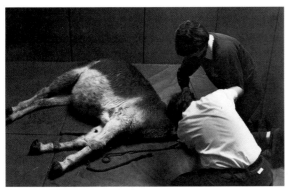

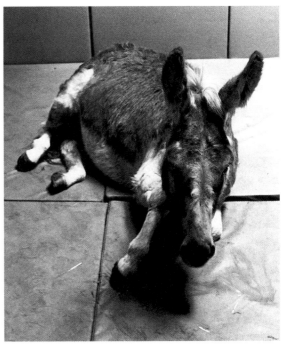

(Left) *Kenny recovering after his sarcoid operation.*

(Top) *Trixie being examined by veterinary surgeon Fiona Taylor before carrying out a biopsy on the tumour in her mouth.* (Above) *Trixie during biopsy.* (Right) *Trixie conscious but not yet standing.*

(Above) *'Jane French is a sympathetic and understanding person.'*

(Right) *Mutual grooming.*

it was malignant or not. If it is malignant her future is extremely uncertain.

Both operations went well and it was nice to come down later in the morning to find the little donkeys in the yard together apparently having forgotten their ordeal such a short time ago.

The behaviour of donkeys has always fascinated me. Keeping them in conditions as we do, even though they are in large units, is not the same as in the wild and I have often wondered whether the strong friendships that are set up here, and the family groups that form and stay together, are a natural part of the donkeys' nature or whether it is something they have developed by force of circumstance. About a year ago we were approached by the University of Bristol School of Veterinary Science who wanted to set up a project for a professional animal behaviouralist to study equines and I felt this would be a marvellous opportunity for a sympathetic and understanding person to come and study the donkeys

under our specialized conditions. Jane French has joined our team for two years to do just this; she is an extremely competent and kind person and seems able to blend in with groups of donkeys in such a way that they recognize and accept her and she can then make her observations without causing any disturbance.

On this particular Wednesday, as on most Wednesdays, we took time to have a chat to see how things were going and what she was finding out. I always find these meetings extremely interesting and today's was particularly so. As you know donkeys have quite loud voices and we have all here noticed different intonations in the bray for feeding time, when they're excited and galloping out in the yard, or just when they see a companion or a human friend; Jane French had decided that she would try to get together some computer equipment to analyse the sound that the donkeys made and to produce a voice print for them. She had started doing this and today she told me of the tremendous difference in the quality of the different brays. One of the most interesting things she pointed out was that in the wild only the male donkeys bray but here the females bray as well. We decided that this was probably an effect of domestication: in the wild mares with young foals keep very quiet as it would be a great disadvantage to draw attention to themselves and to their tiny foals who are very vulnerable. She is now looking into the question of whether donkeys try to convey information about the environment to other donkeys and I will be fascinated to hear the results of her future trials. She also mentioned how much the donkeys enjoyed the sunshine; she had noticed on dull mornings that if a shaft of sunlight appeared through the roof of the barn then as many donkeys as possible would stand in this shaft of light, obviously enjoying the warmth on their backs. In some of our groups, where we have a large number of fairly dominant males, there is also a definite pecking order but again she was surprised to see that a very dominant male who would quite happily push away any other male coming near him would stand placidly allowing any female to feed alongside.

There are many other things that I hope Jane will be able to find out while she is with us so that we can make the conditions even better for our donkeys. We all think we know what's best for them but it would be nice to know that this is what the donkeys would really choose if given the freedom of choice themselves.

Our neighbouring farmer, Mr Hurford, had called in to see me one Sunday to ask if I'd mind if they used one of our fields for access to get to their silage as the front of their farm had been blocked off by the new road construction work at the top of Trow Hill. Living in the country as we do, many of our roads are quite narrow and extremely overstressed during the summer period when the visitors arrive in large numbers. We are also a very short way from the coast at the top of the cliffs and we suffer frequently from a heavy sea mist. This, combined with the notorious Trow Hill corner, had caused a number of fatal accidents in the past and, at long last, the new road scheme to cut the corner was being constructed. We always like to help our neighbours and had willingly given permission for Mr Hurford to use one of our fields known as Smithy as an access. There was, however, one slight problem and that problem was an enormous mule called Jubilee. So this morning, John Rabjohns and I went to the field to look at the fencing.

On January 28th this year amongst the donkeys to be collected by our lorry driver, Perry, was a mule from Matlock. We really had no idea that this was not a normal collection and Perry got the shock of his life on arriving at the address given, with two donkeys already on board the lorry, to find that, in fact, the mule who was coming to the sanctuary was the largest he had ever seen, in fact the largest in the United Kingdom. Jubilee had been intentionally bred by a Mr Robert Way of Newmarket

This one chose just to be loved.

who had worked with mules in the army; it was his ambition to have a pair of large mules. He selected a horse mare very, very carefully; she was called Girl Talk and had retired from racing but was a half-sister to Rubstik, a winner of the Grand National. Having found the mare, he looked all around to find a suitable donkey as a stallion and eventually found one called Eclair, who is what is known as a Poitou donkey. Now the Poitou donkeys have become an endangered species, there are approximately 47 of them left, mostly in France just south-west of Paris, and their future is very uncertain indeed. They are the most beautiful animals, very large and with very long hair. Those of you who know Buffalo will recognize the description and when we were recently

visited by Mr André Phillipe from the Parc Naturel in Poitevin, he declared our Buffalo to be half Poitou. Girl Talk and Eclair were paired up together but, unfortunately, the first foal died. Mr Way then tried again and the second foal was born in 1977, the Queen's Jubilee year, and this is why she was called Jubilee. The mule had aroused great interest, particularly with the British Mule Society, and after her owner was taken ill Caroline Dale, a local horse trainer, was asked if she would look after Jubilee and try to get her into harness. However, it seemed that by the time she was put into training she had already got a little too old to try new tricks and was found to be rather inconsistent.

To the best of everybody's knowledge only

Jubilee and friends.

two mules in the world have ever been bred from; one in China and one in America and many people felt it would be marvellous if Jubilee could be induced to produce a foal and, with that in mind, it was arranged for Jubilee to go to the University of Liverpool Faculty of Veterinary Science to see if it was possible for her to become the first British mule to achieve this phenomenon. However, the original owner decided, having discussed the matter fully with our local inspector, Ron Cox, that it would be more in Jubilee's interests that she be retired to the Donkey Sanctuary rather than undergo the stress of an enforced attempted pregnancy.

Obviously this met with very mixed reaction from the Mule Society and various other people, but Mr Way signed her over to the sanctuary and it was Perry who got the big surprise when he arrived to pick her up.

In view of her size he had to telephone back to the sanctuary and we had to completely alter his pick-up list and advise those waiting with donkeys to be collected that it certainly could not be on this trip, due to unforeseen circumstances. We were all waiting with some trepidation for Jubilee to arrive back at the sanctuary that night, although I must say that John Fowler, our vet who is extremely well known in the horse-world and recognized as an expert, seemed highly delighted at the new arrival. Even having been warned by Perry, we were certainly not prepared for the enormous head that reached out over the box as soon as the back of the lorry was opened and we all realized, with some dismay, that it was going to be very difficult to house her in normal stabling. However, the largest box available had already been made ready and Jubilee was placed in it. She seemed extremely friendly although we all treated her with quite a modicum of respect as you can understand. I went back up to the office, having seen her safely into her stable. My office has a good view right across the main yards and to my absolute amazement, no sooner had I sat down and glanced through the window than I saw the whole stable, in which Jubilee had been placed, erupt and she appeared in the yard with the whole doorframe around her shoulders. Obviously, although completely adequate for donkeys, these doors were not made to deal with giants. Fortunately, she suffered no harm at all and we rapidly changed her accommodation to one of the larger barns where she settled down extremely happily. After finishing her isolation we had moved her across to the field called Smithy, where we were now standing and here she had settled with three mules and a small donkey. We knew, however, that Jubilee would find tractors driving through the field quite interesting and she could certainly appreciate any gates which happened to be left open and the sight of her galloping down the road would be enough to send all our visitors to Devon racing back to their own counties, so we had to make some alterations to the field's fencing. Whilst John and I discussed it, Jubilee stood so close to us that she could rest her big head on my shoulders and the weight was so great that I actually had to move aside, which gives you some idea of the problems we have with Jubilee.

One of the ways of raising funds for the Donkey Sanctuary has been through my writing books, and I started writing children's books some ten years ago, starting off with *Eeyore the Naughtiest Donkey in the Sanctuary*. Ever since Eeyore was born he has made his presence felt. He really was the most amazing foal, always full of life and mischief. His mother, Smartie, had been in the most indescribable condition when I rescued her, so weak she couldn't even stand and I had had to feed her with glucose and water for days on end before she could even find the energy to get onto her feet. She had, however, been pregnant and produced this enormously active foal and during the rest of her short life had a consistently bemused expression on her face as Eeyore thundered round and round the field in ever-

*To prove a point
Eeyore steals the
photographer's lens.*

Afternoon siesta is a pleasure when Eeyore is not in the field.

decreasing circles. One of Eeyore's favourite tricks was to take bobble hats from children standing by the fence watching his antics; there was also one terrible time when a headmistress with a group of children was leaning over the fence with her rather smart handbag dangling from her hands. Eeyore came up to be petted in his usual innocent manner, his eyes the whole time on the handbag and at the correct moment, with a quick snatch, he had it in his mouth and galloped off, round and round the field passing within feet of the now desperate headmistress and her totally out of control and laughing pupils. He had another very clever trick too because in those days we had water butts in every field which were fed by the guttering around the donkeys' shelters. Each water butt had a bung very firmly tapped into the bottom but, unfortunately, it never proved firm enough for Eeyore and another of his favourite games was to get hold of this bung in his teeth and pull and pull until he'd got it out and of course the water supply had gone. Included in his other antics was the opening of gates, at which he became most adept, once letting all the donkeys out of the sanctuary; he has a habit, which he has to this day, of gently butting you on the backside if you happen to walk in the field and do not bother to talk to him. However, I hadn't written a children's book for some time; it appears that many children like to collect these and Julie Courtney, the assistant administrator, who spends a great deal of her time dealing with the public and keeping everybody informed of the donkeys' well-being, had asked me to write another. Jubilee provided the ideal opportunity and I had just written the book called *Eeyore Meets a Giant!*; to my surprise, when I got back to the office, there it was on the table—the first copies in from the printers. Many of the children's books we publish ourselves and it is always very rewarding to see the book completed and I took great pleasure reading this through and seeing the marvellous illustrations done by Eve Bygrave, who has illustrated so many of the children's books.

We now have two lorries used to go out and collect the donkeys from all corners of the UK, both fitted out and equipped to suit the donkeys' needs, but they do the most enormous mileage per week and we were beginning to find repair costs on the number one lorry becoming quite exorbitant. My son, Paul, who had spent years with us running our farm at Town Barton, the farm where hayage is produced, has now changed his job. He decided that if he was really going to be of use to the sanctuary at a later date he should gain experience outside and not at the sanctuary's expense and so he started a small business of his own, in the local area, about twelve months ago. Obviously none of us wished to lose contact and so he has been doing the purchasing for the sanctuary on a part-time basis; he has already managed to save us a great deal of money by standardizing the tractors and vehicles and it is extremely useful to have somebody whose sole job is purchasing, to make sure that the best deal is obtained for the sanctuary, when purchases have to be made.

His experience of running his own farm and knowing the needs of the donkeys proves invaluable but he certainly looked worried when he came into my office this Wednesday afternoon.

Paul, myself and Perry, the senior driver, had spent a great deal of time discussing the new lorry and its fittings and we had been given a promised delivery date. It now seemed this was not going to be met and, obviously, Paul was very concerned about this. It appeared that the current lorry would just have to last that little bit longer and we all hoped that we would be able to struggle through until the arrival of the new lorry.

———————●———————

But siestas can get boring!

THUR

SDAY

Thursday dawned a beautiful day, thank goodness, because this afternoon we've Television South West coming with John Carter who is doing a programme on various resorts in the south-west and wanted to include the Donkey Sanctuary in the Sidmouth feature; in addition to that, we'd the Sunday *Observer* arriving. Ena Kendall who writes articles in its magazine usually entitled 'A room of my own' had asked me previously if I would agree to be interviewed; I had pointed out that I really didn't have a room of my own, my whole life being devoted to the Donkey Sanctuary, but if she wanted to take my office as my room that was fine with me. She was due to arrive that afternoon with a photographer, Christopher Cormack, and they were going to stay all day Friday too, so I had to get on with the office routine fairly early in the morning. I had a quick walk around the yards and found everybody doing very well and no major problems and so went straight up to cope with the post which seemed enormous on this particular morning. I had a meeting with our accountants and Brian in the morning as we seemed to have been having a lot of expense just lately and we have to keep control on everything that happens in the sanctuary. So Brian and I settled down quietly to deal with the morning's mail and try to get through the routine work so that we would be free for television and the *Observer* in the afternoon.

It all sounded a nicely planned and easy day and we had just got started with our accountants' meeting when my telephonist phoned to say 'Oh, Mrs Svendsen, the television company have just arrived.' It wasn't quite a disaster but it was certainly a complete change of direction as Brian had to cope with the problems in hand while I smilingly went down to meet the television crew. They wanted to get some filming done whilst the weather was good. Although the cameraman had attended before,

Visitors photographing donkeys.

(Left) *Blackie happily settled down.*

(Right) *Television crew photographing Blackie with his admirers.*

John Carter had not and he was most impressed as we walked around the sanctuary and showed them our facilities. They were highly delighted with our new foal and decided that was definitely going to be on the agenda and they also wanted some long shots down the drive, with lots of visitors looking at the donkeys and walking around the beautiful walks that we had organized, and also some shots of the children outside the Slade Centre.

The main thing they wanted to photograph, of course, was Blackie. I mentioned in an earlier chapter of the book that we had taken in this Spanish donkey but his story is extremely dramatic. It was last year that we had first been advised of the horrible event that took place in the village of Villanueva de la Vera in Spain where the oldest donkey in the village was used in the most terrible fiesta. The fattest man was put on the back of this poor little donkey who was then dragged through the cobbled streets by a long, thick rope with over 50 knots in it, attached to a very heavy rope halter which had been placed around the donkey's neck. Youths and men each took a place at a knot in the rope and dragged the terrified animal through the village streets. The donkey fell frequently, partly because of the cobbles, partly because of the weight, partly because of the jerky dragging that he was being subjected to and each time he fell he was kicked and poked until he stood again until, at last, they got him to the main market square. Here, for some unknown reason which goes back into the history of the village, the donkey then stumbled and fell for the last time and was then crushed to death by the crowd of people who had dragged him through the streets. At first we didn't believe the story but the production of an eye-witness report, plus the negative of a photograph

The A-team with Blackie on arrival in the UK.

actually showing all the people with just the donkey's leg sticking out underneath, convinced us that this was true. The previous year we had understood that some of the young offenders had been taken to court and we had hoped that this would be the last festival in which the donkey was sacrificed but, unfortunately, events had turned out differently.

Two weeks before the festival was due to take place we had seen a small article in the *Daily Telegraph* advising that the fiesta was about to take place again. We immediately contacted the Asociacion Para la Defensa de los Derechos del Animal, who confirmed that this was, in fact, going to happen. One of the most difficult things was that I was due to go to Ethiopia on the actual day of the fiesta which meant that I wouldn't be able to attend it myself. Negotiations for Ethiopia had taken some time and, going out with a team of four, I felt that I must continue with this urgent project. However, it seemed that a very brave lady called Vicky Moore, from Southport, who was a committee member of the local RSPCA branch, had expressed the intention of going and was not able to get funds from the RSPCA who had decided that they would be better fighting the intended fiesta politically through their many contacts in the Euro-Parliament and in Spain itself. Vicky Moore, however, seemed determined to go and one of our inspectors went to talk to her and rang me saying he thought she would be a very suitable person if we wished to have a representative going on our behalf.

We arranged with Vicky Moore that we would pay her expenses to the sum of £500 to see what could be done to save the donkey due to be killed. The *Star* newspaper and the *Express* were also deeply involved at this stage and Vicky thought she could get plenty of support from the Spanish charity known as ADDA which had connections with the RSPCA. The world press went quite mad. People from all walks of life were horrified at the impending doom of the donkey selected and we were inundated with telephone calls and requests for help. We wrote everywhere, Her Royal Highness, the Queen, Prince Philip, the Spanish Ambassador, in an attempt to get this needless slaughter stopped. We were surprised that the Spanish Government was not able to do more; we had been working in Tenerife and had had great co-operation there from the government in setting up a code of practice which had helped the safari donkeys in Tenerife immensely. The minister concerned was, however, an excellent focal point for me to send the name of all the people who wished to make a protest and we sent over 3,000 during the week before Blackie was due to be killed. As I left Heathrow airport at 6.15 a.m. on the Tuesday morning I read the terrible story and saw pictures of poor Vicky Moore arriving in Villanueva de la Vera with the *Star* and my only consolation was that she was surrounded by press who, hopefully, would be able to take care of her.

I had to leave all the hard work from then on with Brian Bagwell who had the most difficult task of finding out the true facts in Spain and sorting out the press in what became a *Sun/Star* war. Brian is the most wonderful deputy administrator, extremely calm and patient as well as having an excellent business knowledge and sense of justice further inspired by his position as a local magistrate. He was able to sort out the conflicting reports coming in and to cope with the pressures the press began to put on to the charity. Once the *Star* had purchased the donkey they signed it over to the Donkey Sanctuary. Vicky Moore, who had almost been pushed out at this stage by the press, insisted that this was the best place for the donkey to go and, fortunately, the *Star* took her advice. Brian sent John Fowler and Roy Harrington, our senior vet and chief superintendent, straight over to Spain to extricate Blackie from the place he had been hidden and to put him into a safe resting place until we were able to get him back to the UK. He also had to deal with a fanatical *Sun* newspaper which tried to point out various reasons why Blackie should not be brought back to England but be left in Spain. Brian and I had discussed this before I left and we had both decided that if Blackie was saved he could well be victimized if left in that area and we should make every effort to get him back to the UK if this was possible.

John Fowler and Roy Harrington moved the donkey, in the middle of the night, to a safe place and returned to the sanctuary to report that he seemed fit and well except for various rub marks on his neck and sides where ropes had damaged him and some damage to his fetlocks. Brian arranged that a separate account for Blackie's welfare should be opened at Barclays Bank and the *Star* printed this in their

Working conditions in Ethiopia are not always favourable.

paper so that contributions made towards Blackie's keep could be sent direct, an excellent arrangement which resulted in over £13,000 being received into the fund. Telexes flew back and forth to Ethiopia but communications were extremely poor as the nearest telex centre to Debre Zeit was in Addis Ababa and I seemed to receive things a few days after events. However, Brian and Roy arranged that the donkey would stay there safely for the thirty days required, by which time Brian knew I would be home and be able to sort out the problem of bringing Blackie back from Spain.

On my return this was one of my first jobs and Brian and I sat for some time discussing the best possible way. We already had a horse box in Spain but it is a rather small vehicle in which to bring a donkey such a long journey and I was concerned over this. Frequent calls to Spain brought forth little response as to how Blackie was doing but I did get on to the Spanish Embassy to see if there was any way that they could help me in transporting Blackie back to the UK as I felt it might improve relations between our two countries if they were seen to be helping in his return. I give them all credit; they really did try and Air Iberia spoke to me on several occasions. Unfortunately, the largest plane they bring over to England at the moment is the Airbus and the access into the Airbus was not high enough for the crate size we would need to transport Blackie. LEP Transport were also very helpful and offered us a special rate of £3,000 for the air journey for Blackie and ourselves but only on one certain day and, unfortunately, the Spanish authorities were unable to complete his health test by that time. If we couldn't take their offer on that day then the cost would be £10,000 to fly him home and I felt we couldn't spend all that money. We were awaiting the results of the tests but our Spanish agents told us we wouldn't get the final ones until 48 hours before he could leave the country and so, in the end, we had to fix a date when we would go over to pick him up after the thirty days were up.

This meant we had to go over the Easter bank holiday but there was no way out and my team, which I named the A-Team, agreed to go without hesitation. During all the time Blackie was in Spain we had been pestered constantly by phone calls from the press, particularly the *Sun*, demanding to know when we were bringing Blackie home and we were hoping to keep this secret to prevent any problems between the *Sun* and *Star* newspapers yet again. We had agreed to take the *Star* reporters with us as they had, in fact, purchased the donkey and passed him over to us, so they were the only ones in the know when Brian and I finally made our arrangements, although we didn't tell them how we proposed to bring Blackie back, only the date we were going to Spain. Brian and I agreed that we would send our best lorry, specially equipped for transporting donkeys, over on the ferry to France with Perry, my senior driver; he would then drive down to Madrid and meet me there. John Fowler and Roy Harrington would drive over the Shogun which could trail the horse box back and I would fly over with the *Star* newspapermen, be there two days earlier, clear all the paperwork with the agents and then we could all, hope-fully, set off together. The idea was to drive from Madrid to Santander and get the ferry from there to Plymouth which would arrive on the Friday night at 6.30.

As arranged, I flew over with the *Star* news-papermen, Don Mackay and Stan Meagher, and we spent two frustrating days in Madrid whilst I tried to get the paperwork cleared. The agent did not want to be associated with Blackie in case of reprisals after we left and so he refused to put the species 'donkey' down on all the veterinary forms and every other form I required, insisting on calling Blackie a horse. As you can imagine this caused innumerable problems both at the docks and back in the UK, but anyhow I had to accept it in the end. We had been told on arrival to be on the docks at Santander at 4 p.m. on the Thursday, but when I picked up the final papers in Madrid at 5 p.m. the evening before we were going to set off, they then told me we had to be at Santander by 9 a.m. the following morning, so all our plans had to be changed again. Luckily by this time the A-Team had all arrived and we were all together at the same hotel in Madrid. The lorry had travelled over incog-nito, with its Donkey Sanctuary signs inside, and the *Star* newspapermen had travelled with a most enormous suitcase carrying a very thick, red donkey rug with 'Blackie Star' written on it, which they hung on to, grimly determined to use it when the time came.

We left at midnight to pick up Blackie and carefully loaded him onto the lorry. It was a long drive throughout the night to Santander and nobody slept; we were all very tired when we arrived on the dock. We were concerned that the press would spot us on the dock and so having registered our arrival, we moved a short way off and hid the lorry under some large cranes which would give it shelter from the sun and keep Blackie happy. He had travelled extremely well and seemed totally unconcer-ned by the events that had taken place. We then spent nine hours trying to find the papers which hadn't appeared on the dock and it was only at the last minute that we were able to relax and realize that we had actually got Blackie onto the ferry and could settle down for the 24-hour journey.

Our problems were not yet over, however, as by accident the bookings made on our behalf had not gone through and, whilst the men got a cabin for four, I was left with no accommodation. Blackie travelled far better than I did that night. Fortunately the sea was completely calm and the donkey box had been put right at the front of the ferry ready to off-load and eleven polo ponies were in the box next to us, which meant that the deck was left open and we could visit Blackie throughout the night and day as required. Brian and I had arranged that a press release should go out early Friday morning to say Blackie was coming home and would be here at the weekend, without revealing our travel arrangements, which could bring the reporters and upset Blackie. Brian also arranged for someone to phone Vicky Moore to let her know that Blackie was coming back in case she wanted to come to the sanctuary to meet him on the Saturday morning. We all knew it was going to be very late on Friday when we arrived and had hoped that our return would go unnoticed. Our hopes were quickly dashed, however, for as the ferry drew into Plymouth we were informed that the press were 'all over the docks'. Blackie didn't like the last bit of the journey, there were a lot of banging noises from the seamen unlocking the chocks holding the lorries down, and the sound of the reversing engines disturbed him and I spent some time calming him down in the box. The two *Star* reporters were quite determined to put his blanket on, which they did, but not without cost—one had his finger bitten and the other had his foot trodden on.

However, we were all smiling and delighted to be back as we drove down to the customs area. The police and customs men had done a marvellous job and had managed to get all the reporters off the docks and behind the wire. One, however, had crept through and jumped up in the cab with us and started doing an interview. He was very quickly removed by the police but I made quite an error when two more people climbed in and said they wanted to see Blackie and I said, 'Absolutely no way, we are not going to open the doors,' to find they were, in fact, the immigration officials who had to see him. However, all was sorted out and they realized why Blackie had been called a horse and not a donkey and eventually we were waved through. The pandemonium that broke out when we went through the gates was unbelievable. I had told the reporters that we would stop the lorry and open the back door for five minutes but we were not going to allow Blackie to come out and they could just photograph there as he needed a good rest and we were going to take him home. However, one of the *Sun* reporters jumped up into the lorry and actually started a punch-up with Don Mackay which was duly recorded on both television and camera. Quite a return for Blackie, who thought he had got away from all that. Within moments we had closed up the back of the lorry again and drove Blackie home. He was very pleased to be introduced to his new warm stable with an infra-red lamp and something that wasn't moving for the first time in 48 hours, but we were all extremely pleased by the way he had travelled. It was a good night for everybody that night.

Of course Television South West this Thursday wanted some pictures of Blackie and they were very fortunate in that, on that particular day, Blackie had finished the normal isolation he had to have at the Donkey Sanctuary. We had introduced him to a girlfriend called Lola, shortly after he arrived who had come from Wales having herself had a fairly tough life, and they had already made very firm friends. TSW were delighted when we opened the gates and for the first time the two little donkeys, together, trotted out into their own private meadow and enjoyed the lush grass. As the TSW team left happily with their films it was just coming up to 2 p.m. and almost on the dot arrived Ena Kendall and the photographer from the Sunday *Observer*. That afternoon Christopher Cormack walked around, finding his way round the Sanctuary and in fact filmed an operation on one of the small donkeys, while Ena Kendall spent two and a half hours doing her interview.

I always find it very difficult being interviewed; there are so many sides to the sanctuary to talk about, and sometimes those coming down have no idea of the wide range of our work. However, Ena Kendall was completely different. She had done a lot of homework and knew exactly what she wanted to find out and proved a most pleasant person to talk to. She and the photographer were staying the night in Sidmouth so there was no hurry to complete our work and she finally confessed herself satisfied with the interview at about 5 p.m. That night I only had time for a brief round of the donkeys in the yards; it had seemed such a busy day and yet I felt I had achieved very little but everybody was happy and settled and as far as the donkeys went they had had an idyllic time.

———————●———————

DAY

Today was the day that the Sunday *Observer* were going to spend their time taking photographs but I had been extremely concerned by the forecast of the night before. The very low low that seemed to be coming in towards the south-west was increasing in intensity and the forecast was rain, light at first, becoming heavy for the rest of the day, and so I was in at my office desk early to get all the paperwork cleared up before they arrived at 9.15 a.m. Christopher Cormack looked rather miserably around and said, 'Do you think it's going to get any better than this?' to which I happily replied, 'No, I'm sure it's going to get a great deal worse,' and so we began to set up the shot that, no matter what article is done in the sanctuary, every photographer seems to want—that is, myself surrounded by as many donkeys as possible.

Now one of the problems at Slade is that all the donkeys are here for a specific purpose, i.e. they are very old or they are not very well, or they are groups of mares and foals; we don't have very large groups and to get a picture with sixty or seventy donkeys in it means mixing two or even three groups of donkeys normally separated by a fence. Many of the donkeys are very lively and very fit and the chance of a game like this to them is absolute heaven; so when we all stood in the appointed field and the donkeys began to pour in, I wasn't at all surprised when the fun and games started. Because the photographer wanted to get a shot from fairly high up John Rabjohns had brought the Land Rover in and Christopher Cormack climbed up on the tailboard of this and obviously from his safe perch was impervious to the pushing, shoving and kicking that was going on in front of him.

'Stand in the middle of them,' he kept shouting, 'smile at the camera,' and all the time I was being jostled and bumped from front and side. Gradually the donkeys settled down, as we knew they would if we waited patiently and, natural curiosity aroused, they would all gather round as we had hoped. I was doing as asked and smiling happily at the camera without looking around when an enormous blow in the back nearly sent me sprawling on my face. I didn't even have to turn round. 'Eeyore,' I said with exasperation, 'I do wish you'd stop that,' and everybody burst out laughing as, of course, he *was* the culprit. As the photographer started taking his pictures the mist rolled in deeper and deeper until, finally, we could hardly even see the Land Rover, let alone the large group of donkeys, some of whom were still cavorting around the edge of the field, chased, somewhat despondently, by the staff who were trying their best to keep them all in the approved place. Finally, after an hour, he expressed himself satisfied and I would have liked to retreat for a change of clothing as I was completely covered with half-chewed grass and donkey hair, and had a small wet area on my jumper which Eeyore had been happily nibbling during the proceedings, but before I could leave one of our lorries came slowly down the drive containing a load of seven donkeys just arriving.

We all moved up to the unloading bay to see who was coming in and what state they were in. I knew one very elderly donkey who could be in trouble was on the lorry and his name was Ned. He was coming in from the Staffordshire area where he had lived in the same two- or three-acre field for twenty-three years and, sadly, had been made homeless when his owner died. His case had been taken up by one of the local papers and, through this, our local inspector had been called in. The local paper had, in fact, been on to me and kept asking when Ned was due to come in and had done an article called 'Ned finds a home'.

Ned, the Hartshorne donkey, who dug his heels in when his owners decided to sell his field, has found a new home at one of the world's top sanctuaries—thanks to the *Mail*. Next week Ned, who has happily grazed in a paddock off Woodville Road for the last 23 years, will head for Devon.

The move came about after the renowned Donkey

The fog rolled in as the Observer *photographer tried to get his shot.*

Ned coming down the ramp.

(Left) *Fiona Taylor, veterinary surgeon, cleaning Ned's feet out.*

(Above) *Ned in the yard after his lungworm count.*

Sanctuary in Sidmouth read about Ned's plight. The charity's founder, Mrs Elisabeth Svendsen, said today: 'We have a press cuttings service so we knew about Ned. His papers have now been signed and sealed and he will be brought to Devon some time next week. He will be among his own kind and his own age with plenty of space to run about.'

And here was Ned arriving in the lorry along with a very mixed bunch of donkeys. Among this group of donkeys was one whose owner's husband had had a heart attack and the donkey had since been looked after by a young girl and should be in a reasonable condition, two of our rehabilitated donkeys, Dougall and Pedro,

who had originally been sent out to keep a horse company, but the horse had been moved and the family no longer wished to keep the donkeys as one had become rather naughty, and three other donkeys who had come in having been rescued from a proposed trip to the slaughterhouse where they would have been turned into pet food.

The donkeys on the whole were in fair condition apart from Ned who was obviously in need of a little extra care, love and attention. How true this turned out to be as, when we had the results of his first dung sample, Ned had the highest worm count ever recorded at the Sanctuary—over 26,000 lungworm larvae in one sample. Neither Ned nor the other donkeys had particularly bad feet, but for all that, quite a few could have developed problems in the next few months had they not been attended to. Once the donkeys were safely led away to their isolation box I managed to slip home and make a very quick change of my still rather sodden and dirty clothing. Christopher Cormack then spent some time with a little foal who was almost three weeks old.

Flora, Fauna and Boyo had been relinquished from the New Forest in the third week of April this year. As you are probably aware many ponies and donkeys are 'turned out' in the forest and many fend for themselves throughout the year although all have individual owners. The 'agisters', who are the body of people who have responsibility for the care of the forest and its animals, do what they can to care for the livestock, but difficulties arise annually due to extremes of weather or the speed of traffic passing through the forest, with resulting horrific injuries received by the equines. Our inspectors visit the forest regularly and have set up a grading system with the agisters and once a donkey falls below a certain grade, with the agisters' permission we have the authority to advise that it be moved off the forest and returned to its owner for individual care. In this case there were a considerable

83

(Preceding spread) *Every photographer's shot—this one taken by Ian Cook,* People Weekly *magazine.*

(Left) *Little Fern— our new arrival.*

(Right) *Fern on her way to be weighed.*

Flora, Boyo and Fern.

number of donkeys whose conditions were deteriorating and the owners decided that they were having great difficulty in as they call it 'commoning' in the forest and were worried about the mysterious disappearance of foals over the previous years. They therefore decided to let us take two of their mares and a colt into the sanctuary.

On arrival it was quite obvious that Flora was heavily in foal and so she went into one of our special foaling boxes on her own, but in the adjoining box, with a wire mesh between, went the young colt and his mother. While the two

mares were named (Flora and Fauna), we didn't have a name for the young colt. We had just received some very nice correspondence from a doctor living in London who had become the executor of a friend's will. Under the terms of that will the balance of her estate was to be distributed to charity, the selection of which was to be at the executor's absolute discretion. She very kindly donated to the Donkey Sanctuary a considerable sum with which we established two of the walks in the grounds which I have mentioned previously. She also requested that, if it was at all possible,

we should consider calling one of our future donkeys 'Boyo' and so the little colt from the New Forest was named. Flora's little filly was born early one morning during April and, in keeping with the names of her mother and her aunt, it seemed very appropriate to name her Fern. She entranced the *Observer* photographer, who spent ages watching her cavorting round her mother and behaving in the most endearing way.

The afternoon was just as desperate as regards weather and our photographer seemed to have sunk into the depths of despond.

However, our second lorry came in with two little donkeys called Ee and Ore on board. Both these donkeys had been rescued from going to slaughter and the new owner had spent a lot of money trying to get their feet done. The new owner had lost his lease on his rented field and had been given a week to get rid of the donkeys and in view of the emergency the sanctuary lorry had had to turn out urgently to Milton Keynes to collect them. Both the donkeys were in a poor state, particularly with regard to their feet, but they had travelled extremely well and John Fowler, in this instance, decided that they

(Left) *Fern feeding from Flora;*   (above) *Fern on the weighbridge.*

should be corrected immediately rather than leave them any longer. With the photographer watching, he carefully pared the hooves back to the correct shape and immediately eased much of the stress that the donkeys were experiencing from the difficult stance.

Another week had almost gone and as the *Observer* people left in the ever-increasing gloom and the weather closed in with a gale starting up, I walked around the yards for a final time before the weekend. Almost every donkey had decided to come in for the afternoon in view of the rain and the quite cold wind, despite it being June, and all were happily munching at hay or straw, or standing quietly dreaming looking out into the mist from the dry warmth of their stables. The yard staff were doing final rounds and the old geriatrics were

being given their last bran mash for the day, some with carrots and apples added. There was an atmosphere of complete peace and tranquillity, no visitors now, the weather had driven even the hardiest away, and I returned to lock my office feeling a good week's work had been done.

However, a worried looking Mal was at my office asking if I would phone Roy Harrington, our chief superintendent, as we had a big problem and Roy was extremely concerned. He had taken possession of a mule which had been so badly mistreated that the veterinary opinion that he had taken in the area had said the mule would probably have to be put down if it didn't show improvement in a week. The tale he told me was quite horrific. One of our local inspectors was called on the telephone by a

(Above) *The jenny mule found too late.*

(Right) *We could not even get her to the sanctuary.*

member of the public who had been to a dealer's yard to see some donkeys. He was very distressed, not only about the conditions for donkeys but also about the state of about a dozen or so horses and ponies, as well as a jenny mule who was in a sling, having been said to have had an accident while out driving a cart. The dealer who owned the animals was an extremely difficult person but agreed to sell a jenny donkey. The member of the public returned with a friend to collect the donkey so that the friend could also see the condition of the mule for himself and report to our inspector. The conditions were appalling: short ropes and very little room for the animals to turn; mounds of manure which the animals were forced to stand on and no grazing whatsoever available. The mule, over which our inspector was so concerned, was in a horrendous state and it appeared no vet had been called; due to

facial injuries, she had not been able to eat or drink properly since the accident. The man purchasing the jenny donkey was so concerned that, eventually, he managed to buy the mule for £40 and along with our inspector moved her into care. The inspector immediately contacted the office but in view of the description of the injuries of the mule it was suggested that a full veterinary examination should be made on the spot before we arranged to pick her up as it sounded possible that she would not be in a fit state to travel. The vet reported back that the mule had a pronounced cardiac murmur, nerve damage on the left side of her head with resultant muscle paralysis to lip and nostril, she was partly blind in the left eye and going blind in the right, she had teeth missing and the remainder were very irregular. He had rasped as much as possible and had removed the impacted food debris. She was also suffering from severe neglect and fluid imbalance and was certainly not fit to travel. On receiving the report from our inspector, Roy Harrington decided he must go and see her for himself and, as I write this, Roy is on his way. When I spoke to him on the phone I said, 'Roy, surely we can get a prosecution on this to stop people like this from dealing with animals in the market,' but Roy said 'Mrs S., our hands are tied behind our backs—the people involved are quite rightly frightened and dare not be involved.'

It is a very sad reflection that in these days these sort of things are still happening. I keep praying that we have solved the major problems for donkeys in this country; I can accept seeing donkeys abroad in a terrible situation because I feel the owners know no better, but I am not able to accept cases of direct cruelty in this country which is supposed to be a civilized nation. The events that are just unwinding tonight as I finish this book are obviously going to be disturbing and upsetting and I sincerely hope that we are able to solve problems like this and prevent similar events happening again.

We are absolutely determined to prevent the Fiesta at Villanueva de la Vera taking place next year. To this end we have written to every member of the European Parliament one of whom was Mrs Castle.

Our charity is represented on the Eurogroup for Animal Welfare and we were delighted to see that the Rt Hon. Mrs Castle has drafted and tabled a motion for a resolution on Rule 47 in an attempt to prevent such a festival taking place again. Our charity feels strongly that, as well as taking practical action, we should keep our members, able to act politically, fully informed so that we can approach the problem knowledgeably from all sides. Here is the letter Mrs Castle wrote us:

From Barbara Castle MEP
Headland House
308 Grays Inn Road
London WC1X 8DP

2 May 87

Dear Mrs Svendsen
Thank you for your letter of 16th April.

I can assure you I have been very aware of the events surrounding the fate of Blackie the donkey, since I have had over 400 letters from my constituents about the fiesta in Spain.

As an active member of the Eurogroup for Animal Welfare I have taken action to try to stop these fiestas taking a cruel turn in the future. I have tabled a resolution to the European Parliament, and I enclose a copy of a press statement I made at the time of tabling the resolution. I will most certainly not let the matter rest and will continue to do all I can to stop animal cruelty wherever it occurs.

With all good wishes.

Your sincerely

Barbara Castle

We need help, we shall continue to need help for many years, not only from donations, but also support from ordinary people taking the trouble to let us know if they see anything wrong with any donkeys, not only in this country but anywhere in the world, so that we can at least make an effort to put this right.

POSTSCRIPT

Lucy and Katy have now settled in very well but have remained at Slade House Farm in view of their age. They are able to walk normally again and have made great friends with the permanent group of geriatrics and are very contented.

Penny and Tuppence have now gone to one of our other farms, known as Three Gates, where they are able to graze and play over a very large acreage with 400 new friends. Their facial injuries have healed up and the hair is just beginning to grow again, although slightly whiter in colour than before. Both donkeys are now fit.

Jenny, Just William and Lincoln: Lincoln has made extremely good progress and he and Jenny are in a paddock at Slade House Farm with the nursery group. Jenny does not seem to miss Just William at all and is perfectly content and satisfied just to be with Lincoln and the other mothers and their foals. Just William has settled down very well in Buffalo's group and his stallion tendencies seem to have receded completely.

Kenny's operation was reasonably successful. Some of the bigger sarcoids were removed completely, especially the big one at the top of his ear, which now looks rather depleted. However, it seems to be causing him no problems and the others which were removed do not seem to be recurring. Kenny has had to stay at Slade House Farm but is in one of the big new barns which has a run-out of over 3 acres including a small patch of woodland so he is very happy in his new quarters. Emma's Boy is still with him and they will remain until the vets are completely satisfied that there will be no need of further treatment.

Sadly Trixie was not so lucky. We received the dreaded news from the laboratory that the tumour in her mouth was malignant and it was therefore decided by the vets and myself that the kindest action was for her to be put down. Although with our large numbers of donkeys it is obvious that some will die of old age or others have to be put down to prevent extreme suffering, nevertheless I still find this very sad and that particular day was not a happy one.

Blackie looks fitter every day and is still a constant source of interest to the many visitors to the sanctuary. He has completely lost his fear of loud noises and comes happily when called. He certainly does not seem to have had any reaction to the British climate. He will, of course, have special care during the winter with infra-red lamps in his box, which no doubt Lola will enjoy sharing.

Flora and Fern are in the nursery group at Slade House Farm and are doing extremely well.

Ee and Ore are now out of isolation but will have to be kept at Slade House Farm for another three months in case they might be pregnant. The early tests have proved negative but these are not always 100% accurate so we feel they should stay near the hospital until a definite diagnosis is made. They could quite possibly be suitable for rehabilitation at a later date if they are not in foal.

Ned is happily settled at Brookfield Farm.

The very sad news is that the jenny mule, said to have had an accident, had to be put down. Her injuries and the neglect she had suffered caused her condition to deteriorate rapidly and unfortunately help had come too late, except that we were able to ease what would have been a very painful death.

Finally, the good news. You may remember I mentioned Meron Tsegaye, the little Ethiopian girl, whom I brought to England. After over two months of skilled medical care in England, they were able to control the intracranial

Lucy and Katy recovering

pressure by the careful balancing of drugs. Over the last month both her eyesight and hearing have begun to come back and yesterday we were able to send her back to Ethiopia to her waiting family almost fully recovered; with the continued use of the drugs a full recovery should be ensured. Meron became so interested in the Donkey Sanctuary while she was with us that she has expressed the wish to come and work for us when she is old enough and we have promised we will make every effort to get her back to the UK when she is eighteen years old so that her big dreams can be fully realized.

Elisabeth D. Svendsen MBE
July 22nd, 1987